Across From Now

Across From Now

poems
Andy Fogle

GRAYSON BOOKS
West Hartford, CT
www.graysonbooks.com

Across from Now
copyright © 2020 by Andy Fogle
published by Grayson Books
West Hartford, Connecticut

ISBN: 978-1-7335567-9-8
Library of Congress Control Number: 2020903063

Book & cover design: Cindy Stewart
Cover art: © Jacqui Larsen, "Green House, Red Door, Stormy Day"

Marla, Luna, Watson, Penelope, Obie: home.

Acknowledgments

My sincere thanks to the editors of, readers of, and other contributors to the following publications where some of these poems first appeared:

Binnacle: "My Father Calls During my Daughter's Bath"

Blackbird: "Crossing Mourning Kill" and "Nine Martinsville Screens"

Broadkill Review: "Cobla at Midnight, 17th and Boardwalk" and "A Train Can't Look Back"

Cutbank: "Motel Across Lincoln While I Pump Gas"

Mid-American Review: "Field Trip"

Natural Bridge: "The Corner Insists It Is the Place," "Non-Sequitur at Saratoga Battlefield," and "One August Back in Falls Church"

Naugatuck River Review: "July 1978"

Parks and Points: "Sunset for Now at Naples, Florida"

Poetry South: "Triptych Compromise"

Roanoke Review: "'Many Years Ago We Parted from the Sunny Mountainside'"

So to Speak: A Feminist Journal of Literature and Art: "One Ring"

South Dakota Review: "Lake Tiles" and "Rising to a Wedding Across from Mt. Hood"

Still: The Journal: "Five Lights" and "Thinking of Virginia in New York"

Unbroken: "White Whirl"

William and Mary Review: "How to Ride the Ferry from Waterside to Portsmouth"

Thanks

Among teachers, I'll go all the way back to first grade at Kempsville Elementary School and offer gratitude to Ms. Walker. For their later encouragement and kindness at Kempsville High School, I put my hand over my heart and nod to Elaine Denson, Kevin Denson, Ms. Cupp, Barry Graham and Ruth Pleasants. For their guidance, patience, generosity, example, and friendship at George Mason University and beyond, I send much love to Peter Klappert, Carolyn Forché, Eric Pankey, and Jennifer Atkinson. Most of all, also at GMU and beyond, Evan Oakley. He probably squirms at my calling him the most important teacher of my life, but it's the truth.

Among friends, for their commentary on versions of this manuscript, and the required eyes, ears, intellect, and intuition: Mark Fitzgerald and Hope LeGro. There are dozens of other friends and colleagues over the years that have nourished me and, directly or indirectly, my writing, but I will emphasize the love of Jeff McKinney and Nikhil Ranade, because we have traveled so many miles and made so much noise together.

Among family, there are similar dozens, but I must highlight my parents Connie Lynn Brown Fogle and Paul Woolley Fogle, III for their laughter, tolerance, and toughness, and my grandmother Lorene Fogle for her seemingly endless endurance and the wild magic of her stories.

Here at home, the dogs—first Luna, and now Obie—brought me into a larger world.

The kids, Watson and Penelope, are full of more wit, wonder, wisdom, and weirdness than I imagined possible, and my imagination is right potent.

For all of the above and more, my wife Marla: teacher, friend, family, home, love.

Contents

Field Trip	11
One Ring	12
July 1978	13
A Mile West a Creek, a Mile East a River	14
My Father Calls During My Daughter's Bath	15
Motel Across Lincoln While I Pump Gas	16
"Many Years Ago We Parted on the Sunny Mountainside"	17
The Road Home	18
Nine Martinsville Screens	19
Thinking of Virginia in New York	29
Crossing Mourning Kill	33
Sunset for Now at Naples, Florida	35
Popham Beach	36
Cobla at Midnight, 17th and Boardwalk	39
Five Lights	40
White Whirl	42
Triptych Compromise	43
Ten Hallways in May	44
Seven Father-Screens in Horse Pasture, Virginia	46
Object Permanence	53
Lake Tiles	54
Rising to a Wedding Across from Mt. Hood	56
How to Ride the Ferry from Waterside to Portsmouth	57
Notes on the Poems	60
About the Author	61

Field Trip

According to a museum placard, the jack pine's serotinus cones need fire-hot temperatures to release their seeds, and so can reproduce intensely after a forest fire.

This upstate pond is where Jilliana catches the biggest baby sunfish anybody has ever seen in their eight years on the planet, and where tadpoles feel like jello. Under the mama crayfish's tail, it's packed with tiny purple beads like grapes: her eggs.

This is where Ava gives me her drawing from the museum, signs it on a picnic table in the pavilion.

I doze on the bus, both ways, but catch one kid cry, upon arrival, "We're here!," and when we leave, "We're going back in time! Goodbye, future, we'll miss you!"

This, the world my son has brought me to, is where Sam C. made out just fine without his hiking boots, white birch like a statue of ash popping among dark hemlocks.

This is where Isabella picks a dozen blue wildflowers on Green Trail Spur, between two forests where you can see the lake called by the Mohawk, Onandaga, and Iroquois *where the lake is closed in by mountains*, or the *lake that shuts itself in*.

According to the placard, the jack pine can reproduce intensely after a forest fire. Because of the fire.

One Ring

Back when phones still had bells inside them
and plugged into walls, back when we were
tethered to the box, we'd get home

from Poppie's, and Ma would call, let it ring
once, and hang up. This gone all-clear signal,
a call cut short, unanswered, no talk,

and the worried father an hour away
could listen, count, and breathe easy
at the nothing that followed a little.

July 1978

The day before my mother turned 30, her mother died. A week later, my dad working a night shift at the warehouse, she felt safer with me in their bed until he returned. She was calmly crying.

>But I saw her mother stroll
>our backyard, touch azaleas,
>admire rosebushes, inspect
>tomato plants, so I said,

Don't worry. She'll be back.   *She'll be back.*

No, she won't, honey.   *No, she won't.*

Disregard pronoun antecedents,
deprioritize clarity—one? Both?

Either? It was all the same

mother in the clock radio's orange
glow, time's tiles quietly clicking along.

A Mile West a Creek, a Mile East a River

Two weeks after the hospital,
picking Draper blueberries,
the short bushes are fullest.

Grandma Brown used to say,
*You gotta bend it back
and get right in there like this.*

Amidst broken hearts and blindness,
another grandmother
nursed her dying daughter.

I was the one to phone my father
with news of his father's death.
He'd been in a good mood—*Hey,*

boy!—then speechless against
the loading ramp's plangent wash.
These are not the natural

orders of things. Beyond the field's
far corner, the Bacon Hill
Reformed Church is ringing.

My Father Calls During My Daughter's Bath

He's on the side porch open
to the south meadow, as a storm
booms through. Do I remember
running to him? *Daddy, Daddy,*
can we go sit in the garage
and watch the storm? I'd help him
put the door up, and we'd sit
in lawn chairs, feel the thunder
in the floor, watch water rush
down Amberly Road. She squawks
in my face, he cackles in my ear,
and I span to heed the arc
that beams and fades and crackles again.

Motel Across Lincoln While I Pump Gas

An oil tank in the bed
of their big white pickup.

Like dolphins arcing
through surf in unison,

two men outside a room
raise cans to their lips.

A third in a lawn chair lights
one up. His cupped hands,

a tiny fire, a tiny cave.

"Many Years Ago We Parted from the Sunny Mountainside"

On the east side of I-
81, sunflowers are jading,

but still tall as me.
On the west side, three silos,

empty now, but much taller.
After hours amidst

the armada of semis,
I must be tripping—just

rectangles and cylinders
floating south along the highway.

The map abstracts terrain,
reduces distances, makes

of water and wood
ink, obliterates

texture, yet preserves
like little else. Can I so

recreate white haze
on the dark eastern ridge?

Not so much. Only the names
retain the touch of place:

Buffalo Gap, Mint Spring,
Hornet Road, Dooms. Some deaths

sprawl long as an official
blowhard's speechification;

others are quicker
than snapping a string bean.

The Road Home

I propose to Marla that Virginia glares more than New York, that the light is sharper. Adirondacks' green is a softer shine, she speculates, because it's farther north, we get less direct, more glancing, sunlight. Southern Virginia's summer glaresky all white haze, yellowed palefrost, assault of erasure. And yet the Adirondacks' white-blind winter compares, its color-drought, its cast-over empties, its driven-down face. Two places one, the glares of opposite seasons—the things your driving guessworks at.

                      Gushing from woods
                      to roadside, a doe
                      and two fawns. Miles
                      later, the buck alone.

Nine Martinsville Screens

1.

All three are true of here: the state's poorest city in the state's poorest county, which also has the highest percentage of millionaires in the state.

    Eastern tiger swallowtail among vincas—

Splintering swing
in a line of walnut trees,
my daughter's wild hair.

        The toddler names the action
        as it is done, the just-past
        rendered in the present tense:
        I eat the grapes. I spray
        the hose. I fall down.

2.

The twice-two-timed wife
two-timing two men,
one from before she met
her twice-two-timing husband.

        My father to his
        sister about their
        mother: Why was I
        never told these stories?

Tomatoes ripen on the windowsill—

    That dead oak's
    like a giant cactus.

3.

She came home once to find her three grandsons had filled the crepe myrtle with action figures, clothespins, scarves. Story was, it looked like a band of gypsies had moved in. As the years unfolded, this turned out to have some truth.

> Crepe myrtle's way:
> almost as soon
> as surfacing,
> the trunk divides.

After high school, the oldest one moved with his girlfriend from Germany to Colorado, and it didn't take long for things to dwindle and verge. Walking home after a graveyard shift at 7-11, he got jumped, mistaken for someone else.

> Crepe myrtle bark—
> easy to peel,
> quick to stab.

The middle one was *so quiet you wouldn't even know he's here.* Once he drank a pint of whiskey and stopped by her house before heading downtown to meet his father and friends at a hockey game.

> Fill, fret, flee—
> a dozen blackbirds
> in a scrubby myrtle
> little bigger than you,
> its limbs like bone
> the color of lime.

The youngest one spent a nomadic summer with two girls, backpacking, hitching, often hungry. One morning in a village on the Mediterranean, someone bought them a baguette. On the way down to the sea, they picked somebody's strawberries. He floated naked on his back, glimpsed the girls doing the same. Later, on the empty beach, they ate the berries, and they ate the bread.

4.

I sucked at subtraction in second grade, so after awhile, Mrs. Morris sent a note home. In my parents' bedroom, my father addressed it with me, while I lay on their bed and cried, staring into the ceiling light. *Well, tears are good for your eyes.*

        Another porch beer—
        waiting for night
        to fall into place.

5.

    Buzzards loop far above
    the carcass, and memory,
    likewise, I'm sure.
    They twirl like searchlights,
    beckoned and strung.

Whoever has come to know the world has discovered a carcass, and whoever has discovered a carcass is worth more than the world.

    From trough to crest,
    from topsoil to dustcloud,
    the arcs and coils confound.

    Is *this* the same person who—

        Love baby, love baby,
        that's where it's at. That's
        the faded red spray paint
        on the yellowed cinderblock
        of the B&R Appliance Store.

6.

Downstream of the Fieldale Bridge,
Canadian geese
loiter the jutting rocks.

> The arm that guided my own
> now guides my son's. How to draw out
> the thick green glowing line, the growing
>
> back-and-forth arc, the same length ahead
> as behind. How to track the fly
> in its flight, dip, and swirl, to know
>
> what is stream, to know what is strike.
> The arm that guided my own now guides
> my son's. I never really learned.

One thing it's about is patience with what looks like nothing, the tug you feel but are yet to see, the presence in what is fluid, and what is present in the stream.

> The swollen leather of my father's hands,
> the minnow's lithe and silver gleam.

> Let me know what to preserve
> and what to discard,
> what to hang and what to sing:

> > *The river*
> > *where you set*
> > *your foot just now*
> > *is gone—*
> > *those waters*
> > *giving way to this,*
> > *now this.*

7.

>   To break the power of the past,
>   boil nine black walnuts
>   still in their husks
>   and bathe in the brown tea.

They say in Franklin County, you can walk down any creek and find an old moonshine still. *Heat, cool, condense. Vapor that peoples, vapor that swoons, here's to the spirits that make the head spin.*

>   On the west side of 220 North
>   to Roanoke, ambassador
>   of peace and fertility,
>   a doe squats to piss.

8.

Against white azaleas, an eastern comma's black flash—
at the center of its wings, a tiny orange throb.

    The black wooden ball of a rotten
    walnut, unfetched, ruined by webworms
    in the first place, O wayfaring purpose.

           If damaged by sunburn, drought, or husk fly—

    So many branches
    of so many trees,
    bound by the mist

    of fall webworms' nests—
    and they're all over
    the tent we pitch

    as we pitch, as we talk
    into a fire, as
    we sleep and wake.

9.

> As tears brim—"You *are*
> a good man"—
> meteors shower
> generations.

How much can you lose at once? One October, when a plane crashed into Bull Mountain, killing all ten aboard, Rick Hendrick lost his only son, his brother and his twin daughters, three close friends and business partners, another friend, and the two pilots.

> Massive stream of debris
> in the Perseids' 133 year orbit—
> my father's halfway there.

No Business Mountain is reputed to have been home to an inordinate number of moonshiners and rattlesnakes. Which one sprung the name depends on who you're talking to, but either way, the line is the same: *Boy, you got no business on that mountain.*

> Midnight piss—one meteor's
> green murk, long and thick,
> slashing up the sky
> beyond the roof of the barn.

Two cousins talk family in the 4am driveway, while directly overhead, Perseids. One's flash, almost painfully white, longer than its streak, like a tear with no trail.

Thinking of Virginia in New York

1. Meditation on a Big Muff Pedal

Clockhand with limits,
compass with a blind spot,
the sustain knob goes
to 5 o'clock, the far
southeast, and holds the note,
prolongs the chord. Never-
mind distortion, I don't
know how you do it.

2. Thinking of Virginia in New York

Seeing the dead, mind guides itself
into anti-, considers an ice dam's
cycle of melt-freeze-melt-freeze.
Already the birthplace is gone.

The soul is the mind's fault, the mind
the body's, on up and up the list
of signatures, tangled in breakneck.

If I am the whore of nosotrostalgia,
then seagulls divebomb the dark beyond
the surf. Leave the water in the muck.
Stopwatch the tripped-out ripples.

A grist of phone calls swirls above the bay.
The salt-foam glazes, settles into grit.
Them seagulls mingle, nibble on trash.

3. A Bus Stop in Fairfax

To wait for that to
make it here to take me
there—to kill time
in the meantime.
Bluecloud claws

in the near-dusk sky,
saw-toothed leaves
and splayed elm cough
in wind's torrents. The sun:
off, sky still streaked with it.
The road knows where
I'm going, have
been, doesn't
care. *When? When—*

4. The Corner Insists It Is the Place

A certain time of day
gathers about the capitol,
sun moaning down to skyline,
and the past comes skipping
back: leaving a hospital
in a strange city, glad to be free

of my dying relative, sick
for that gladness. The gutters
drink the dregs of rainwater.
Just below, that which gurgles
gurgles. 14th & H—for now,
a whirlwind of the working

soon on their way home. The same
at night, empty but for
the homeless. New rainclouds heave
along the city's fringe, metallic
smell, the swelling air, the *here*
that needs not note, is both

consciousness and coma,
unrapt, unfelled, the here
that clamors and swirls, tips
and turns desolate,
nothing for our absence.

5. One August Back in Falls Church

Post-epic-yardwork, second skin
of sweat-grime, slugging cold beer
in the shower. Why these things come back
like this—beyond me. From a distant
thought, I hear myself set the bottle
on the tile, sound and steam tumbling
out the window into pink sky.

6. "This Painting I Like Because You Can Get in There and Rest"

The moon comes to our window later and later each night, and we take pleasure in checking it out, but this part's far away, Clinton Avenue in Albany: I remember an ivy-covered brick building wavering in pre-storm wind. Coming rain smelled good, and it felt good for it to smell the same as it did in childhood. Since sometimes to track what passes is (I'm afraid) more than enough for this me, that was probably one I should've been grateful for, when it was what it was. We might be here longer than we think.

7. Non-Sequitar at Saratoga Battlefield

Now that I've read the marker (how many
dead), the deer are spirits for sure. White
scribbles up from the distant woods and a trail
of gray leaks down. If the base of things
is slick and green, rock and dirt, the pinnacle
must be mist. Does here look so from there,
this open hill, those lower, denser woods?

The deer watch me the way I watch the dead:
startled into waiting, curious
for the other's first move. The sandy deer,
the lower woods—I'll never see here
how they do. Unlike that mind, this one hungers
otherness, demands it to make ends meet.

8. Me Voy

Dogwalk after dark,
you crane your neck,
the now and then tiptoe
to glance into glowing
spaces hovering in the night,
and imagine your life inside
the inside you imagine,
like paging through the latest
issue of *Nostalgia*, with,
you know, "bittersweet yearning,"
blind hand in your pocket,
as with each new image
your breath quickens.

9. A Train Can't Look Back

Where're the ones we were? Don't know about that.
For an hour straight, threads of lightning thrashed
and flumed, glittering blue salt, sting of sour mash,
fading down, down the line. First the voice, next the rumble,

then the light. Call time. Oily midnight,
deeplit gloss where nothing grunts and coos, state
the slippery unwinding, swing the smoke and echo,
loose the steam and hiss, make it with my made-up mind.

Crossing Mourning Kill

Sift the roots of disease—

Pissing evil,
a drafting compass—
to go, to come,
to stand or walk
with legs apart.

To see without the center,
to speak through cracked lips.

To grip with the hands or teeth,
to grasp with the mind.

The mark of a pen,
the striking of a clock,
the single pull of an oar.

*

No way out through words,
only the momentary stays,
the usual discovery,
litany of awes and ails.

*

My boy's three year check up
three months overdue.
The rain, and August's sinny vegetation.
Route 50 South to Burnt Hills,
the pleasure of signs and names,
directions and numbers.
Modest, pitiful facts,
amidst passing faces.
Just killing time? Can't say.

*

A few days before Christmas, my father's mother. A few days after, his best friend. Fishing in March, he scrambled from the river during a lightning storm, and broke a bone at the bottom of his shin. From the steep bank back to his truck, a half-mile crawl though the flashing world.

*

The popping knees, one roughed-raw;
the calf-cramp that spiders away;
azien, short breath, a panting;
a single abnormal kernel;
the enlarged veins resembling crab legs;
the spreading sores hard as crab shells.

*

When road transverses creek,
when now is filled with then,
when the living look to the dead,
when we dwell in the palace of grief.

*

A catch,
a holding,
possession.

An old woman's
last word: *always*.

Disappear,
be born.
Amiss? Arise.

Sunset for Now at Naples, Florida

Check, check. All the standard elements
are here: sea-sky horizon, the small-shelled
shore-lip, scattered palms, a happily
zig-zagged pier, a boulder jetty
that works for now. It's like walking through
a photo album: a father holding
his small daughter, then hands with his wife,
who later chase-stalks her son. The whole
family of four, framed by these tokens
and an aging man's squint, who is three things
to these four people—father, father-
in-law, grandfather—and his tremor
does not for now. Pan the scene: a group
of twenty-somethings timing their leap
for the camera on a tripod; a man
with a construction company t-shirt
teaches his son to surf; smokers fume
on the wood steps leading from lot to sand;
retirees in lawn chairs with coolers
of boxed wine and cutting boards. In a few years,
some of these kids will be big, some of these
elders ash, and vice versa. They've gathered
to witness another day pass. The air
is stable and clear, the light less scattered,
so when the sun slips, they glimpse the green flash,
treasured mirage, and then, for now, they all applaud.

Popham Beach

Somewhere out there's
a place we
call to and, in
calling, quake.

Unslaked,
unshapened
up, I say
in place.

*

Twice a day, low tide exposes sandbars.
Twice a day, high tide obscures.

Our wannabe selves, released by the sinking,
then marooned on Fox Island by the rising.

*

Once into her twenties, she cut off her family. She would occasionally see her brother, but never her parents, and although as they withered she did start sending Christmas cards, even when her father was on his deathbed, and she was offered a flight home, she replied, *That time has passed.*

*

The beach changes each year as the river feeds and feeds,
as a line of water to the south greens,
as the sandbridge builds beneath the surface
and one lagoons another to shallow and walm,
as the outgoing tide wavelengths the shore.

*

Lobster steamed in a jug's worth
of seawater reddens because all
the other pigments leave their shells.

*

What power the heard-of
has on the known,
and the unheard-from
has on who's home.

*

Toward the mouth of one,
but at the mouth of another,
to found and abandon within a year,
the lighthouses I didn't see,
the foghorns I didn't hear.

*

After walking down the driveway to get his mail, and then back uphill, he was more winded than usual, so my father drove himself the 20 minutes to the hospital, where the experience was classified an "episode."

*

My boy's tooth loosens
without anyone knowing.
When he loses it
at a rest stop, he will be
proud, because loss means
you're becoming big.

*

On the way home from our friends', we'll stop off at a baby shower, and the hostess, the expectant mother's mother-in-law, will remark on all that is *incredible*.

*

My girl runs like a drunkard
to hug my knee, hair
a black flash of slime.

*

Recovering from cancer, he caught and released six brook trout.

The fish we keep? Once broiled, the flesh releases the bone.

Cobla at Midnight, 17th and Boardwalk

The rain has stopped, two kids make sandcastles,
and on a hotel's fifth floor balcony,
she screams at him. The broken branch
of lightning spans the sky, then doesn't.
On a bench in the wind, a ten-year-old boy
in a coloring book's maze. Next bench down, a man
beside a brown paper bag, hands clasped
across belly, chin on chest. A small
blue shoe soaking wet beneath a streetlamp.
Make, scream, color, sleep. Does, then doesn't.

Five Lights

The backyard swing a rare space of pendulum
intimacy. It was just the nearby
car dealership extravaganza-ing
the dusk, spotlights twirling the sky, but Dad
said, *I think a giant in heaven's lost his dog.*

*

Before we had an air conditioner,
we'd sleep flip-flopped, our heads at the foot
of our beds, to better catch the breeze

oozing through the windows. I remember
a helicopter's spotlight sweeping
the neighborhood—Ma said they were looking

for a runaway kid, and when the beam
lit up the squares of my windowscreen,
I worried the runaway might be me.

*

All around our block, a fine blend
of January fog and chimney smoke.
The flashlight's beam gropes and scans
tree-undersides, a pillar of luminous
steam. Shine it directly on the sky
and something stops it, definite and unseen.

*

Janaf, Pembroke, Military Circle,
somewhere or other, I withdrew
from the movie and sought its source, above

and behind us: tube of light twisting
from the projector like a swimmer.
It spread into a cone, larger

and paler near the screen, where the story
assembled, and all the heads enrapt:
tilted back slightly, collective, inverted bow.

*

Guilfoyle and Wojcik invite students
to huff the new projector screens. Up close,
the surface is white and scaled, and the chemical
divine. It won't last forever, this newness-buzz—
over the years, the aromatic skin
will be worn by light, by images of ourselves.

White Whirl

My mother makes friends with husband-and-wife dance instructors, and stays friends for 25 years until a falling out with the wife who two years later is dead of a brain tumor, but when I'm thirteen they have a pool and a hot tub, and I go over with my mother where sunshine abounds, where they've never had any kids of their own, and at thirteen it's glamour to be allowed in the hot tub by myself thinking of girls at school and of doing things with them that my father did with another woman, living it up, the way my mother now lives it up out dancing at clubs, comes home smelling of smoke, dates a series of men for a month each, or goes to her friends' pool, where she never swims, not because she doesn't want to, but because she can't.

Triptych Compromise

At night, creatures seek safety under weed and rocks
but the ray scans for them, ten feet above.

If you choose my sanctuary, leave the drive hidden.
Am I speaking loud enough? How's the mix?

*We're gonna angle off the edges of the peninsula
cuz y'all can't agree on anything anymore.*

Tellin' you, we transform God through live words,
as a corolla spider labors behind a grain of quartz.

*

The man with the heart of a child heads out the door.
Deep inside the cloud, not because of anything.

Suggestions there's something wrong with the house
prowl the limp daylight. Who is he? The father has no son.

They come like music from hollowness,
like mushrooms from damp.

Just like you, gutters worn out by stormwater.
Just like you, spitting image, as they say.

*

Only your eyes and hands to point the way,
only the pre-dawn memories to sit the now beside.

Since my habits have had it with one another,
whenever consciousness decides to begin,

I just hope my palms can stop reading shit into
each other's every movement. When the raincloud begins

its licking, and the air is full of no-telling, Mother Tongue
and Father Foot, what have you to do with one another now?

Ten Hallways in May

Riding with Dad one evening to pick up a load of wood, he asks about my day.

"We played Girls Chase Boys today, and I didn't let any of them catch me. I was too fast for them."

"Well, that's fun for now, but one day, you might *want 'em* to catch ya."

Call me when you get this.
Between my palm and the steering
wheel, gravity strains the popped
blood vessel: two women
drink and smoke on a front porch.

Warren's wife was Buddhist, and he told of a ceremony for a nephew's birth, and what weeping there was.

The oak blossom—
                what
she gave us yesterday,
straight from the roadside
tree—
        still on the dashboard.

I'm 42 and the receptionist might be 30, but she still calls me Sweetie. One day, I'll want them to catch me.

Other patients'
stranger-ness
still shudders me,
as it did when
I was a kid:

        "I don't want the food, I don't want the food"—

"Is someone ever going to come help me? I have breast cancer and need a woman to help me get dressed"—

"She thinks she's going home," laughs an attendant—

Remember the tornado that came through Amberly Road? Your dad said it was only a jet. Dropped our shed on Wanda's and our fence out back. I asked him the next morning, "Did a jet do this?" She tells me this anytime a tornado is mentioned. Decades.

The woman who gave you life—
this speaking that scares me—
her answer to marital
status is "happily divorced."

On Opposite Day, when greeting, two friends say goodbye.

Seven Father-Screens in Horse Pasture, Virginia

1: The Night of Arrival

*We are definitely
burning one tonight,
now that you here—*

Later, he'll stalk the pit's perimeter, adjust logs, offer play-by-play narration. If the pitchfork and wood drag on each other just right, there will be a low ring.

*The wind must've caught something
just right to whistle like that.*

Every beer's the last beer, then another set of waves. *Hold on, now. In a minute I'll tell you a funny story.*

*Rising's how sparks die—
they settle and fade
on your gray t-shirt.*

Meanwhile, by the porch, unbeknownst to us at the fire, a piece of an old woman long gone unfolds in the night-blooming cereus, meaning *waxen*, so-called from its shape, which suggests a candle.

2: Memory with Cut-Up

Long ago, he said, "You embarrassed her and you embarrassed me. I think you felt like you'd been hurt and wanted to hurt something back." It took a decade for me to see that. Last week I argued with my son, tried to convince him to watch how much pain motivates him, and it doesn't do any good now, either.

    Which mountain is that?
                Chaos.
    When did you start smoking?
                Because I didn't love her anymore.

3: Two Long-Ago Dawns

One morning 40 years ago, we laughed in their bed as I wriggled out of a headlock.

Rumpled sheets. The cotton of his t-shirt on my ear. The warm skin of his bicep on my ear. His beating heart on my ear.

Time has not quelled the play-growls.

> Another morning forty years ago,
> his one day off: *Oh, I'm beat.* Months
>
> of two warehouse jobs, all hours, slow
> to rise. *This old bed feels so good.*

4: Fishing at Illum's Pond

The cows low, the geese
call, and the sound
I can't quite figure
is likely a frog.

He strips line, mutters
to what he can't see.
From the bottom of his
throat, *Show yourself.*

5: Memory with Textbook

Do you hate me for what I've done?

(It took him a month to ask the question,
and me a decade for the admission.
That was long ago.)

Lets go:
        a. Release.
        b. Forgive.

Let's go:
        a. Hurry up.
        b. Hurray me/us! (Common hotshot sports parlance.)
        c. Not good enough.
        d. Join me.

6: Another Night of Arrival

Parish declares,
"I got a hunnerd
count Eastern Seasides
on ice in the car"—
*(You steam 'em on
the grill and they open
right up. Oh yes.)*

and Travis snagged
a big dark red slab
of tuna caught last
night sliced this morning
and brung it five hours
west to let go
two minutes on grill

pinch white salt pinch black
pepper we eat it
still a little cool
inside I can feel it
like watermelon
like grapefruit like all
these things in my blood

7: Go-Figures

Zoe sings, *Sometimes I long to be where I'm from.*

    Presence
        without awareness
probably
        ain't witness.

One dusk he was trimming trees with a chainsaw on a high stepladder when a limb took a funny dip and sent him, the ladder, and the chainsaw falling. He said he lay there afterwards, ladder to one side, saw to the other, unable to move. He said he looked up at the treetops and stars, felt sleep coming on and thought, "Well, I guess if I wake up I wake up, and if I don't I don't."

        As the first step
        into still water
        is murkied by silt,
        sparks swell against quilted
        abdominal clouds.

Object Permanence

She puts the plastic cup
upside down in the drawer
of hand towels, closes it,

reopens, and delights:
still there. Stayed put.

We think "Of course!"
yet just for now. That
was then and there, but

then again, even here
and now, among all this

this-and-that, odd ends,
it isn't gone, although
it's disappeared.

Lake Tiles

Rowing into wind-wake
the hup and slap
of hull and water
all over each other.

> All because of a blue
> dragonfly's draft:
> a worn oar slips
> from its wobbly lock,
> time cuts loose,
> a bubble pops.

Decades ago, my father as a boy at Fairy Stone, the water cold, and Johnny Cash driving the air: *I keep a close watch on this heart of mine. I keep my eyes wide open all the time. I keep the ends out for the tie that binds.* Just a few years back, entering the park, he hops out of the car, springs into the gift shop, returns with a magic stone for my wife.

> Take off this hat
> in August heat—
> the past is and
> the future will
> be fine without
> my attention
> on this here-breeze.

The stones were formed when a messenger brought news of the crucifixion. The fairies wept, and their tears crystallized into crosses, possession of which is protection against illness, accident, or curse. *For you I know I'd even try to turn the tide.*

> Conduit
> for skin and air:
> water smeared
> on face in Back Pond.

They were formed by heat and pressure such as was present millions of years ago during the formation of the Allegheny Mountains. Similar stones can be found all over the world, but nowhere are they more abundant or strikingly cross-shaped than in Stuart, Virginia. This combination of iron, silica, and aluminum known as brown staurolite, which crystallizes in the shape of a cross.

> Drifting way out
> in the middle to snack,
> almonds and cranberries
> are good, but Oreos
> are blessings.

Fifteen yards east of us, a loon dives. We wait for it to resurface, but minutes and minutes pass. So we turn west, and there it is, now forty yards away, bobbing along. That's what we gave up on.

> Now I hear what I saw:
> red-stemmed lily pads
> hiss along the hull.

Love that frets love,
whirligigs zag
the surface we zig.

Rising to a Wedding Across from Mount Hood, Oregon

From the chairlift's center pole
a strand of gossamer
waves in sunlight.

>On the opposite
>coast, her black hair
>silvers my chest.

This morning, walking a tightly-wooded neighborhood's hills threaded with acrid smoke, the sweat came, and the hangover passed.

>As we dip and swell, lull and slip,
>moss grows on a boulder
>and the tips of Douglas firs glow.

At certain elevations,
the temperature swoons.
The ceremony all sky.

>I touch her neck, she
>closes her eyes. Quicken
>at the glimpse of skin.

After the alpine slide, the attendant with tiger stripes tattooed on his head will high-five me.

>Palm to palm and breath to breath,
>back home, goldenrod fills
>the late August woods.

How to Ride the Ferry from Waterside to Portsmouth

1. You can face where the ferry's taking you, or where you are leaving. The former is ploddingly grand, while the sexy thing about the latter's how your future glides over your shoulders, and then appears, first in your periphery, then your central. So you gotta weigh the merits of slow zoom versus come into view.

2. Because, although the former is familiar, sooner or later, the latter just joins all the other stuff, loiters one way or another, however I turn, sliding all around me, out of sight, but in touch. So enough about how we face; it's your call.

3. I don't know if traveling west is into the future and east to the past or now. One might put off death, the other wear it well.

4. How many deaths, or near-deaths, and how many almost-lives. Blocks away, the deadliest part of Tidewater, but here, a tentative recovery, the willful thinking of gentrification. Then? Again.

5. But if I walked there again—the thought alone makes me picture catching my breath on a streetbench. That's what a past will do to you.

6. If you maintain an internal life all your life, you will be troubled and awed by such things. You will have the sense of the isolated everyday marvel, as if clinging to the bottom of a swimming pool, looking up at the sun wobbling far, far beyond.

7. Wind might rise to your tongue, or waves slap the hull, especially if you look straight down over the rail, and if you hold your mind just right, the temporal surfaces and slips everywhere in little pyramids and pits.

8. Let me put on my glasses so I can hear you better. Let me sit around a table with strangers and share strangeness, let me stand up straight home right this second place finish.

9. Story up, and question me a listen. Store this tell before bedtime, ever-after my close-ups. Stare me dawn, blow me downside, the mouth of the port wavering river, Elizabeth's voice, rippling in winter wind, shanked if your head isn't just so.

10. From one downtown to another, we leaned on the rail, smoked, had hot chocolate. I can still feel the ferry's heave, but have no memory of other passengers or the return trip, only going to and being in a place I'd never gone or been. Can you fill it?

11. Answer me when I'm speaking to you. Amberly Road bike spokes soft-clicking cycle of tongue-tussle. Touch me in the night-time, in this night-time right here. Cupping my hand to my ear helps collect the sound.

12. The other downtown is all but vacant though shoplights glimmer on cobblestones. But they're not cobblestones; that's just romance. Turns out the patterns have plain names anyway: diagonal basket weave, herringbone, fishscale, radial, pinwheel, inlays, running bond. That's what a past is: a darkshining dream, empty but for you, and you, and you.

Notes on the Poems

"Many years ago we parted from the sunny mountainside" is from "My Clinch Mountain Home" by the Carter Family.

The two italicized portions of "Nine Martinsville Screens" are, respectively, from "The Gospel of Thomas" in *The Secret Teachings of Jesus: Four Gnostic Gospels*, translated by Marvin W. Meyer (Random House, NYC, 1984), and from *Fragments: The Wisdom of Heraclitus*, translated by Brooks Haxton (Viking, NYC, 2001).

"I like this painting because you can get in there and rest" is a comment made by Agnes Martin in "The Untroubled Mind" in *Agnes Martin* by Barbara Haskell (Whitney Museum of American Art, NYC, 1992).

"Crossing Mourning Kill": Mourning Kill is the name of a small body of water in Saratoga County, New York, with "kill" being Dutch for "creek."

About the Author

Andy Fogle was born in Norfolk, Virginia, grew up in Virginia Beach, and lived for a decade in Northern Virginia, teaching for the DC Creative Writing Workshop, DC WritersCorps, and George Mason University, where he earned a B.A. in English and an M.F.A. in Creative Writing. He has been an educator for over twenty years, and now lives in upstate New York with his wife and two children. He teaches in the English Department at Bethlehem Central High School and is a doctoral student in Curriculum & Instruction at SUNY Albany. Fogle's poetry, non-fiction, and co-translations with Walid Abdallah have appeared in *Anomaly*, *English Journal*, *Gargoyle*, *Image*, *Popmatters*, *RHINO*, *Teachers & Writers Collaborative*, *Writer's Chronicle*, and elsewhere. He is the author of six chapbooks; the most recent is *Elegies and Theories*, published by Presa Press.

www.ingramcontent.com/pod-product-compliance
Lightning Source LLC
Chambersburg PA
CBHW071321080526
44587CB00018B/3312